ARM CANDY

First edition published for the United States and Canada in 2015 by Barron's Educational Series, Inc.

Copyright © Pavilion Books Company Ltd 2015

First published in the United Kingdom in 2015 by Pavilion
1 Gower Street
London
WC1E 6HD
All inquiries should be addressed to:
Barron's Educational Series, Inc.
250 Wireless Boulevard
Hauppauge, NY 11788
www.barronseduc.com

ISBN 978-1-4380-0715-1
Library of Congress Control No.: 2014956701

Printed in China
9 8 7 6 5 4 3 2 1

LAURA STRUTT

ARM CANDY

FRIENDSHIP BRACELETS
TO MAKE AND SHARE

BARRON'S

CONTENTS

INTRODUCTION

It's so simple to arm yourself with some pretty beads and a few other craft supplies and start making beautiful bracelets for yourself, or as gifts for your friends. You could even hold an arm candy party for your besties, making your bracelets together. The materials you'll be using aren't particularly valuable, but the time spent and the gift of friendship they signify will be truly treasured.

You'll find that the projects are easy and quick to make, even if you are trying out a new technique like the loom-band design. Suggestions for color combinations are shown in the photographs, but you can get creative with your own color choices if you prefer.

As well as designs that feature the usual jewelry materials and findings, there are projects made from common crafting items like embroidery thread, washi tape, and spray paint. So if you have any of these materials in your drawer left over from other projects, you will be able to use them up. There are even no-cost projects that make use of recycled materials, like the T-shirt Yarn Bracelet.

So gather what you need and get crafting!

CHEVRON FRIENDSHIP BAND

Woven friendship bands are so much fun to make. Before you know it you'll have mastered this technique for making neat little woven knots and you'll be whipping up a stack in all your favorite color combinations!

YOU WILL NEED

> EMBROIDERY THREAD, IN TWO COLORS

> SCISSORS

> SAFETY PIN OR WASHI TAPE

CUSTOMIZATION TIP

Create wider bands or add in more colors by simply increasing the number of strands of embroidery thread you use, keeping to an even number.

USE A SERIES OF SIMPLE LITTLE KNOTS TO CRAFT A COLORFUL COLLECTION OF WOVEN BANGLES

1 You will need four embroidery thread lengths in color A and four lengths in color B. Trim the lengths to around 80 cm long. Knot the lengths together 10 cm from the end.

2 Divide the short lengths above the knot into three sections: two with three strands and one with two strands, and braid from the knot to 2 cm from the end. Knot the threads together at the far end of the braid to secure. Insert a safety pin into the knot—or use a section of washi tape—and secure to a firm surface (you can use a cushion, ironing board, or even the leg of your jeans).

3 Spread the threads out and arrange them so there are, from left to right, two color A, four color B and two color A threads. Separate these threads to create two halves, each with two strands of thread A outermost and two of thread B innermost.

4 To create the friendship band you'll work lots of little knots. To make a knot, bring the first thread over the second, passing it under and bringing the end through the loop.

5 Draw up closely to tighten the knot into position.

6 Repeat step 4 to make a second knot with the same threads in the same way. These two knots count as one woven stitch on the bracelet. Begin the chevron. Take the threads on the far left and create one woven stitch (see steps 4, 5, and 6) on the thread to the right-hand side of it. Continuing with this thread, repeat to create another woven stitch on the next thread and then the thread following it. The initial thread will now lie at the center of the strands.

QUICK TIP

Be sure to draw up each of the little knots you make (see steps 4 and 5) to create the chevron pattern neatly and tightly. This will help to create an even finish to the friendship band without any holes or gaps in the woven stitches.

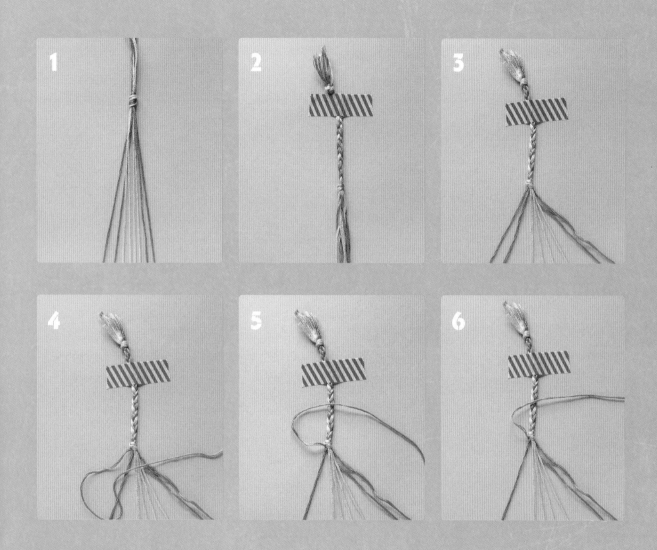

7 Complete the point of the chevron. Make a single woven stitch over the next three threads to end in the center. Join the point of the chevron by working the two inner threads together with one woven stitch.

8 Begin making the second half of the chevron. Return to the outermost thread on the left-hand side and repeat to create three woven stitches to reach the middle of the section. Then work three woven stitches from the right-hand side to meet at the center and join the two center threads with a single woven stitch. This will create the first V in the chevron pattern in thread color A, with each one being made up of two lines of woven stitches meeting in the center.

9 Begin the second chevron. Take the threads on the far left and create one woven stitch (see steps 4 and 5) on the thread to the right-hand side of it. Continuing with this thread, repeat to create another woven stitch on the next thread and then the thread following it. The thread will now lie at the center of the strands.

10 Moving to the other side, begin making the second half of the chevron. Make a single woven stitch over the next three threads to end in the middle. Join the point of the chevron by working the two inner threads together with one woven stitch.

11 Return to the outermost thread on the left-hand side and repeat to create three woven stitches to reach the center of the section. Then work three woven stitches from the right-hand side to meet at the center and join the two middle threads. This will create the next V in the chevron pattern, with two lines of woven stitches in thread color B.

12 Continue working steps 6–11 to repeat the chevron pattern for the desired length. Tie a knot at the bottom of the bracelet to secure the woven design. Divide the thread into three sections—two with three strands and one with two strands—and braid to 2 cm before the end. Tie in a knot at the bottom to secure and trim the ends neatly before tying to your wrist or gifting to a friend.

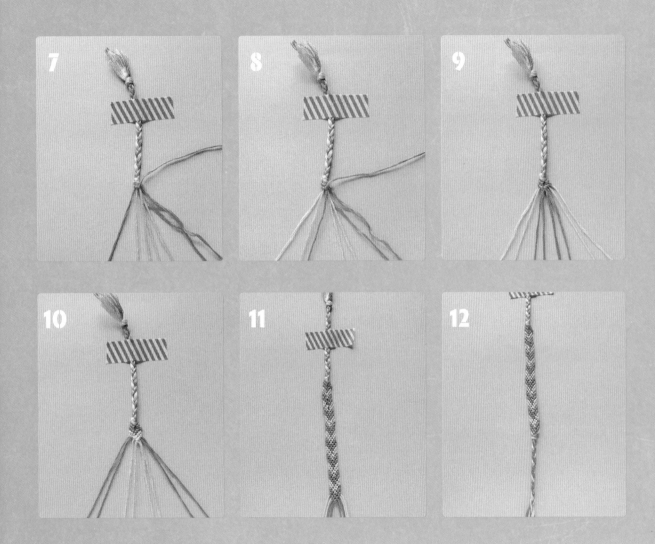

CHARM MOTIF BRACELET

A large charm in a graphic flower shape makes a great focal point for this simple statement bracelet. Team it with colorful cord, and you'll create a finished result in no time.

YOU WILL NEED

> MEDIUM BOOTLACE CORD, IN TWO COLORS, 40 CM OF EACH

> SCISSORS

> CHARM OF YOUR CHOICE

> FOLDOVER CORD ENDS X 2

> SLIM FLAT-NOSE JEWELRY PLIERS X 2 PAIRS

> JUMP RINGS X 2

> BRACELET TOGGLE CLASP

CUSTOMIZATION TIP

Pick any statement charm with large open sections—these will work best as they give you a section through which to thread the cord. Try using a purchased heart or star, or even make your own openwork shape from jewelry wire.

CREATE A STATEMENT BRACELET
WITH A LARGE CHARM

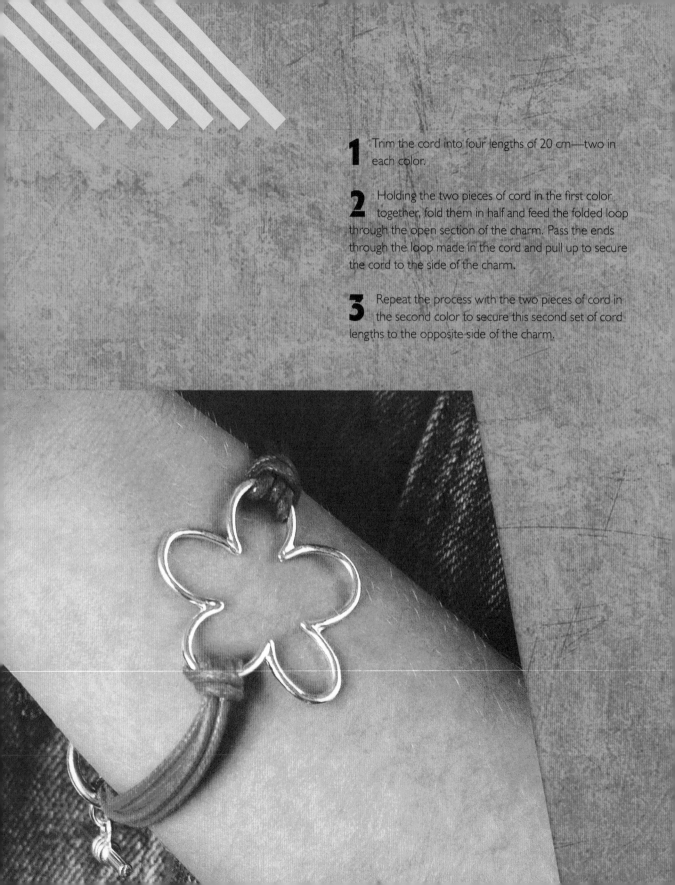

1 Trim the cord into four lengths of 20 cm—two in each color.

2 Holding the two pieces of cord in the first color together, fold them in half and feed the folded loop through the open section of the charm. Pass the ends through the loop made in the cord and pull up to secure the cord to the side of the charm.

3 Repeat the process with the two pieces of cord in the second color to secure this second set of cord lengths to the opposite side of the charm.

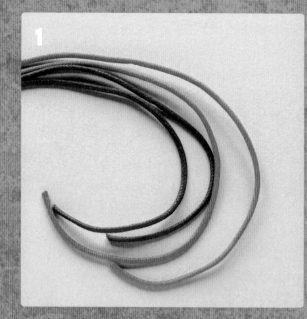

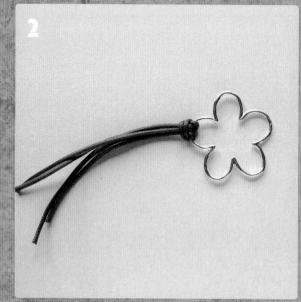

4 Working on each side in turn, secure the four ends of the cord into the cord ends, folding over and pressing them closed with one set of the flat-nose jewelry pliers.

5 Use both pairs of jewelry pliers to twist a jump ring open (see tip). Slide the ring through the loop on the first cord end and then through one end of one half of the bracelet clasp. Twist back to secure.

6 Repeat step 5 with the second jump ring to secure the second part of the bracelet clasp on the opposite side of the bracelet.

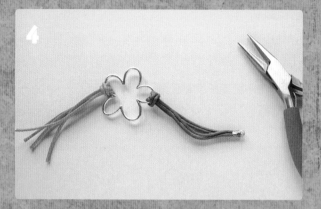

QUICK TIP

When opening jump rings to secure the clasp, work carefully. Twist the two sections apart by holding the ends of each section with a set of pliers held in each hand, then rotate the pliers away from each other. By twisting the rings apart, rather than pulling them open, you will be able to close them back neatly—just reverse the twist process to restore the original perfect circle shape.

T-SHIRT YARN BRACELET

Cotton jersey ribbon yarns are great for making colorful, soft accessories. Why not use old T-shirts to make the yarn yourself and create new arm candy at zero cost?

YOU WILL NEED

> T-SHIRT YARN (OR T-SHIRTS CUT INTO STRIPS)

> SCISSORS

> SEWING NEEDLE AND THREAD

CUSTOMIZATION TIP

Make a chunkier bracelet by using six strands of T-shirt yarn. Hold the yarn strands in three sets of two, and work the braid in the same way as the three-strand version.

UPCYCLE OLD T-SHIRTS TO CREATE STUNNING BOLD BRACELETS

1 Cut T-shirt yarn—or strips from old unwanted T-shirts—into 30-cm lengths in multiples of three different colors, shades, or designs.

2 Knot one end of a set of three strands of yarn or T-shirt strips together and spread out the free lengths neatly, ready to braid.

3 Create the braid by taking the strand on the left-hand side and bringing it over to the center of the set of three strands. Move to the right-hand side and bring the strand in toward the middle. This creates the braid.

4 Continue braiding the strands by bringing the outermost strands in toward the middle in turn.

QUICK TIP

Create your own T-shirt yarn by cutting old unwanted T-shirts into 3-cm wide, 30-cm long strips ready to be braided.

QUICK TIP

Strips cut from T-shirts, or T-shirt yarn, can be very stretchy. Pull and stretch the lengths of yarn slightly before braiding so that the bracelets won't stretch as you wear them and become too large.

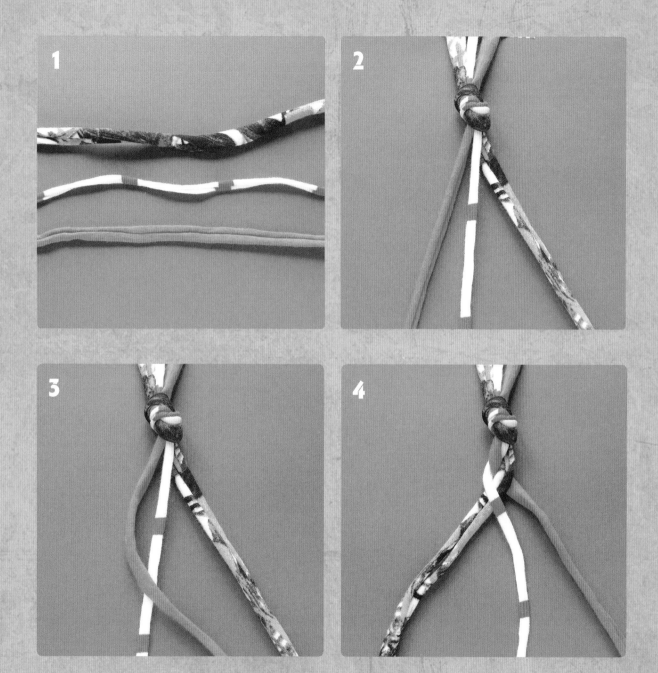

5 Continue working the strands together until the braided strip is 4 cm longer than the circumference of your wrist.

6 Using the needle and thread, work a few stitches through the base of the braid to secure the ends in place, knot securely, and fasten off. Remove the knot from the other end of the braid and work a few stitches through the strands to secure the braid on the opposite end. Knot securely and fasten off.

7 Trim five of the six ends of the strands to 2 cm from the end of the braid, leaving one strand untrimmed. Without twisting the braided strip, overlap the two sets of shorter ends and, with the needle and thread, work a few stitches through the join to secure the braid in a circle. Knot securely and fasten off.

8 Wrap the remaining (untrimmed) strand neatly around the join to conceal the ends. With a needle and thread, work a few stitches to secure the wrapped section on the inside of the bangle to finish. Knot the thread securely and fasten off.

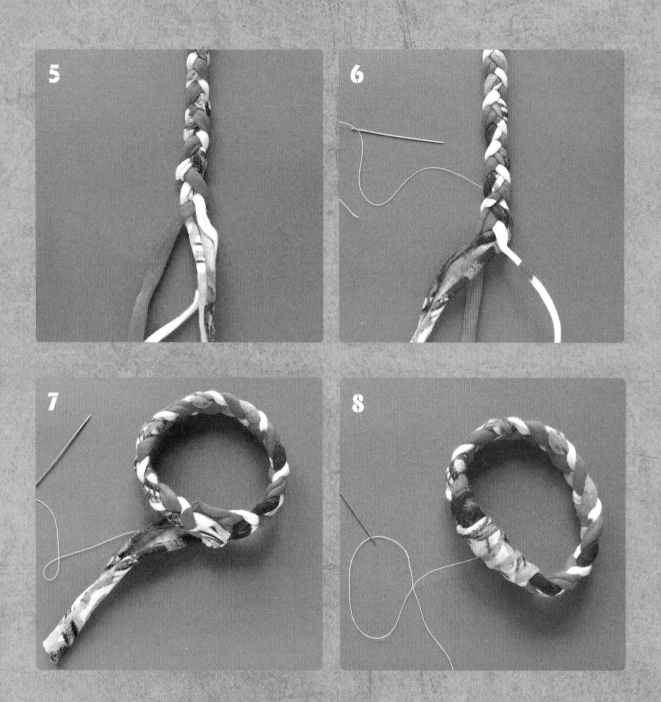

WASHI TAPE BANGLE

A paper crafter's favorite, washi tape comes in a huge range of prints and colors. Pick your favorite combinations to create your own statement bangle.

YOU WILL NEED

❭ OLD WOOD OR PLASTIC SMOOTH-FINISHED BANGLE

❭ SELECTION OF WASHI TAPES

❭ SCISSORS

❭ MOD PODGE DECOUPAGE GLUE (OPTIONAL)

CUSTOMIZATION TIP

Create a metallic effect by using silver duct tape, adding pieces in the same manner as the washi tape. Or cut shapes and accents from duct tape to add a custom finish to your bangle.

CUSTOMIZE OLD BANGLES WITH WASHI TAPE FOR A FRESH NEW LOOK!

1 Clean and dry the old bangle. Plan your design using a collection of washi tapes in complementary designs.

2 Cut the washi tape into small strips slightly larger than the width of the bangle. Working around the bangle, begin securing the tape onto its surface. Fold the cut edges neatly in toward the inside of the bangle, and make sure that each strip is fully adhered before adding the next.

3 Continue covering the outer face of the bangle with tape strips, overlapping them slightly to make sure that none of the original bangle is visible.

4 Cut two strips each measuring 3 cm longer than the inner measurement of the bangle. Carefully secure the first strip around the inside of the bracelet. Repeat to add the second strip. If the bangle is very wide, you might need to add a third strip so that all the cut edges of the folded strips are neatly covered and secured.

QUICK TIP

Washi tape is quick and easy to apply. You can reposition the strips as you work if you are not happy with the placement. However, the more you remove and reapply the strips the less sticky they become, so make sure that they are fully stuck down before moving on to the next strip.

QUICK TIP

For longevity, seal the finished bangle with a coat of decoupage glue (mod podge) or matte or shiny clear varnish to protect the tape from dirt and damage.

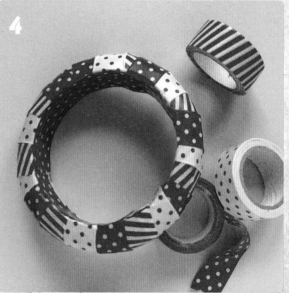

URBAN KNOT BRACELET

Impress your friends with your clever knotting technique—this chunky cord bracelet is surprisingly easy to make. Try out different colors and thicknesses, then stack for a cool armful.

YOU WILL NEED

> MEDIUM PARACORD, 3 M

> SCISSORS

> CRAFT GLUE

> PLASTIC SNAP-CLIP CLASP

> WASHI TAPE OR STICKY TAPE

CUSTOMIZATION TIP

Paracord is a lightweight nylon rope originally designed for parachutes, hence its name. Initially it was made only in natural and olive drab, but today there's a rainbow of hues to choose from. You can even buy the cord in neon colors and a glow-in-the-dark version that would make great bracelets for night owls on a mission!

DISCOVER HOW TO CREATE A STRIKING URBAN-STYLE BRACELET WITH THIS CLEVER PARACORD KNOT DESIGN

1 Cut a 75-cm length from the cord. Apply a small dab of craft glue to both ends of the cut length and those of the remaining piece to prevent them from fraying. Set aside to dry. Fold the 75-cm cut length of cord in half and feed it through the opening of one half of the clasp. Push the cord loop through from front to back, then draw the ends through the loop.

2 Secure the clasp in place with a piece of washi or sticky tape. Center the remaining length of cord and tie in a knot around the secured cord, making sure that the knot is fastened snugly to the base of the clasp. Position the lengths of knotted cord on the outside. The cord secured to the clasp will sit in the middle.

3 The knots are created in two parts. You make the first part of the knot by passing the left-hand piece of cord under the center two pieces and the right-hand piece of cord over the center two pieces. Feed the cord from the left-hand section up and through the loop made by the cord on the right-hand side, and feed the cord from the right-hand side down and through the loop made by the cord on the left-hand side. Draw up to tighten the first part of the knot.

4 Create the second part of the knot by passing the left-hand piece of cord over the middle two pieces and the right-hand piece of cord under the middle two pieces. Feed the cord from the left-hand section down and through the loop made by the cord on the right-hand side, and feed the cord from the right-hand side up and through the loop made by the cord on the left-hand side. Draw up to tighten the final part of the knot.

QUICK TIP

Be careful when using glue: avoid contact with your skin and work in small dabs at a time to make sure that it is not visible on the finished bracelet.

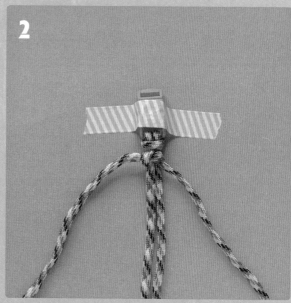

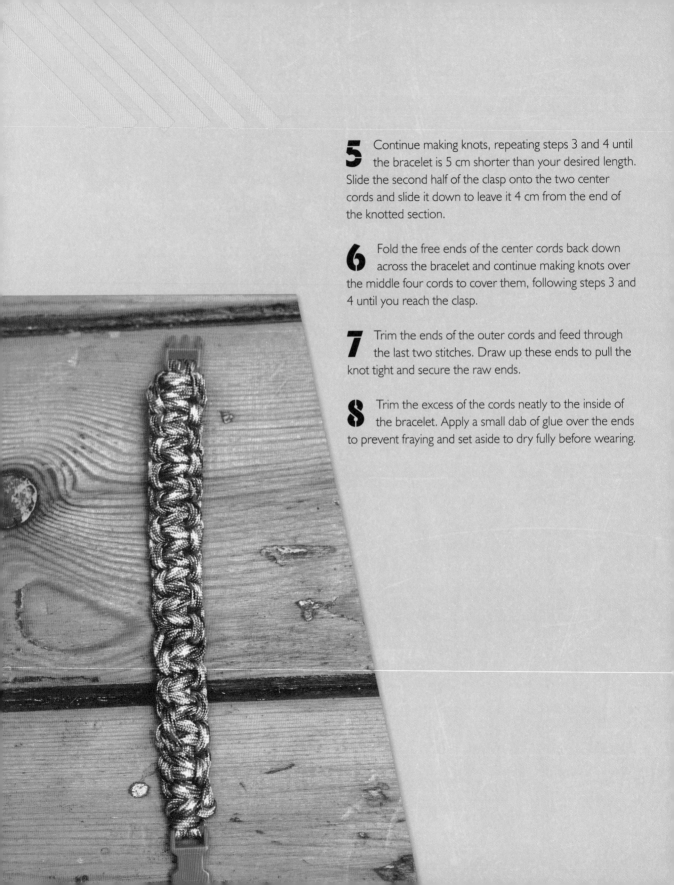

5 Continue making knots, repeating steps 3 and 4 until the bracelet is 5 cm shorter than your desired length. Slide the second half of the clasp onto the two center cords and slide it down to leave it 4 cm from the end of the knotted section.

6 Fold the free ends of the center cords back down across the bracelet and continue making knots over the middle four cords to cover them, following steps 3 and 4 until you reach the clasp.

7 Trim the ends of the outer cords and feed through the last two stitches. Draw up these ends to pull the knot tight and secure the raw ends.

8 Trim the excess of the cords neatly to the inside of the bracelet. Apply a small dab of glue over the ends to prevent fraying and set aside to dry fully before wearing.

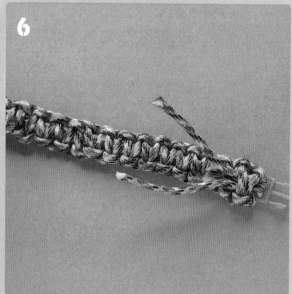

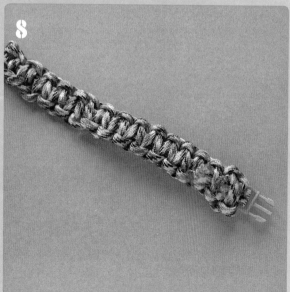

CROCHET BEADED BRACELET

Adding a scattering of bright little glass beads to a simple crochet chain worked in twine is easier than you might think—and makes a stunning festival-style bracelet.

YOU WILL NEED

> NATURAL TWINE

> SCISSORS

> GLASS BEADS, 4 MM (25–35 BEADS, DEPENDING ON WRIST MEASUREMENT)

> WASHI TAPE

> CROCHET HOOK, 5 MM SIZE

CUSTOMIZATION TIP

Work with a random selection of colored beads for a unique finish, or pick a couple of your favorite shades and create a repeated pattern for a more coordinated design.

COMBINE NATURAL TWINE AND COLORFUL BEADS FOR TRUE BOHO STYLE!

1 Cut a 1-m length of twine and begin to thread on a selection of beads in your preferred order. Hold the other end of the twine down with washi tape to prevent the beads slipping off if needed.

2 Add a knot to one end of the twine and slide two beads to the knot before knotting again. This forms one of the ties for the bracelet.

3 Measure 10 cm in from the inner knot and knot again. At the base of this knot tie a slip knot and insert the crochet hook through the knot, drawing it up around the hook. Use the hook to catch the tail of the twine, and draw it through the slip knot—this is a crochet chain stitch.

4 Slide the first bead to the base of the crochet chain stitch you just made, use the hook to catch the tail of the twine, and draw it through the loop on the hook to make the next stitch.

QUICK TIP

If you are using larger beads, be sure to pick a larger crochet hook, too. Select a hook that is 1 mm larger than the chosen beads—so, if you are using 5-mm beads, use a 6-mm crochet hook.

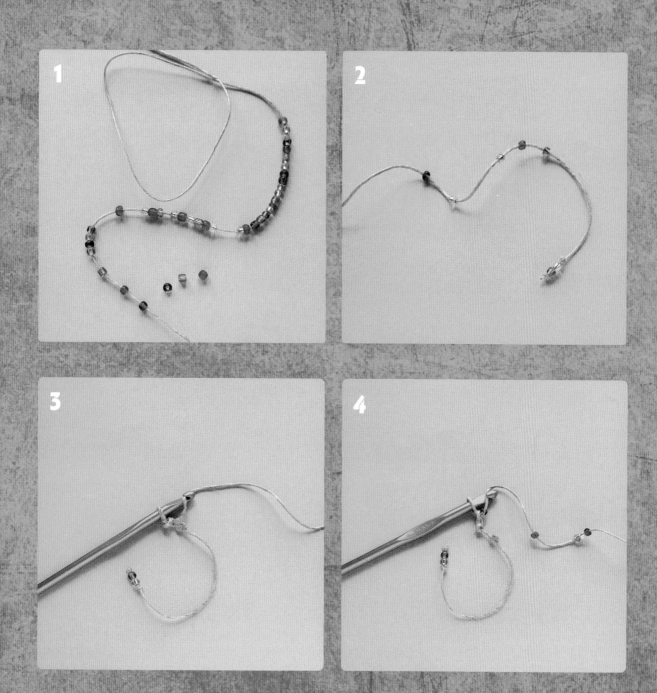

5 Continue sliding the next bead on the twine onto the base of the crochet chain stitch you have just made before catching the twine with the hook and drawing it through the loop on the hook.

6 Continue to make the crochet chain, adding beads at each stitch until the worked length is 2 cm longer than your wrist. Remove the hook and tie the twine in a knot at the base of the length of beaded crochet chain to secure. Make sure that there are two beads left on the remaining length of twine to make the end of the tie.

7 Measure 10 cm along the twine from the base of the crochet chain and make a knot. This will create the second tie.

8 Slide the two remaining beads to the outermost knot and secure in place with another knot above them. Trim away the end of the twine below the outermost knot to neaten, and knot the ties into a loop to finish the bracelet.

QUICK TIP

Threading the beads onto the twine can be a little tricky. Make sure that the ends of the twine are cut neatly, as frayed ends are harder to feed beads onto.

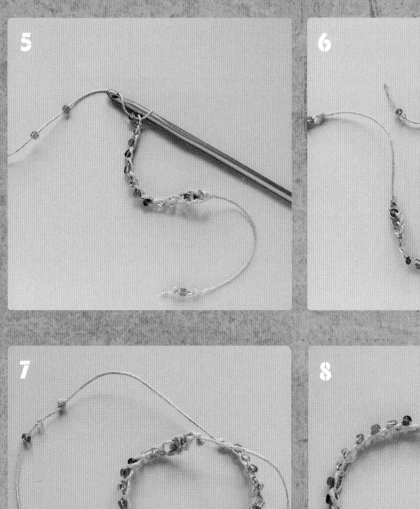

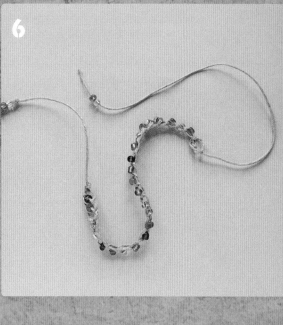

BEADED SAFETY PIN BRACELET

Make a statement accessory that your friends won't believe is made from simple safety pins embellished with tiny beads. Use one, two, three, or a rainbow assortment of colors to vary the results.

YOU WILL NEED

› SAFETY PINS – MINIMUM 60

› SEED BEADS, IN THREE COLORS

› THIN SHIRRING ELASTIC

› SCISSORS

› WASHI TAPE

CUSTOMIZATION TIP

Instead of threading tiny round seed beads on the safety pins, why not try using the long type known as bugle beads for a different look?

TRANSFORM EVERYDAY SAFETY PINS
INTO A STUNNING BRACELET
WITH DOZENS OF SEED BEADS

1 Open the safety pins and feed the seed beads onto the pin. Once the pin is full of beads, secure the safety pin closed. Repeat to fill 60 safety pins with seed beads—30 of each color of beads.

2 Position the safety pins in the order needed to create the design using the three colors. Make sure that the safety pins are each positioned in opposite orientation to the one next to it—one with the opening end upward, the next with the coil end upward. This will help them stack snugly when secured together to make the bracelet.

3 Cut a length of shirring elastic 20 cm longer than the measurement of your wrist and thread through the upper section of the row of beaded safety pins. Make sure that the elastic passes through the top section of one safety pin and the bottom part of the next, with the beaded section facing out.

4 Cut a second length of shirring elastic to 20 cm longer than the measurement of your wrist and begin threading it through the lower section of the row of safety pins. Slide the safety pins up neatly and snugly together as you work, being careful not to slide them off the other end of the elastic.

QUICK TIP

Secure the ends of the shirring elastic to the table with a piece of washi tape. This will stop the safety pins from sliding right off the length of elastic as you feed them into position.

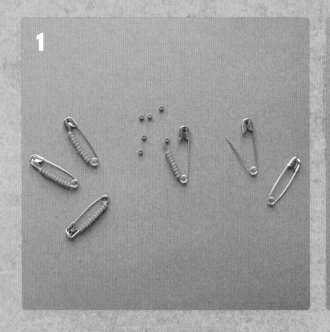

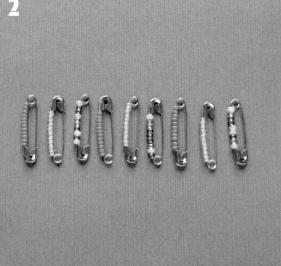

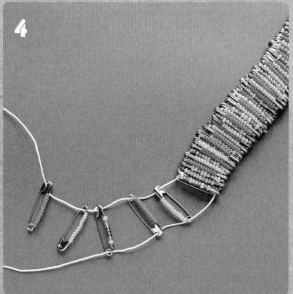

5 Holding the ends of the elastic, draw together the upper length and tighten to form the bracelet. Knot the ends together securely and trim away the excess elastic.

6 Draw up the lower length of elastic to complete the bracelet, secure tightly with a neat knot, and snip away the excess elastic.

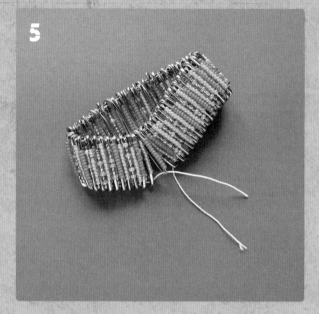

QUICK TIP

Be sure to work carefully when using safety pins, as the pin ends are very sharp and can cause injury.

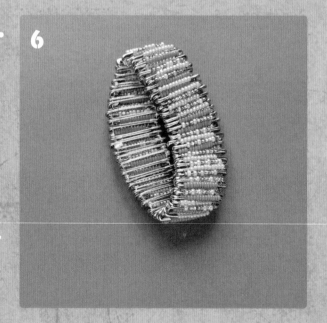

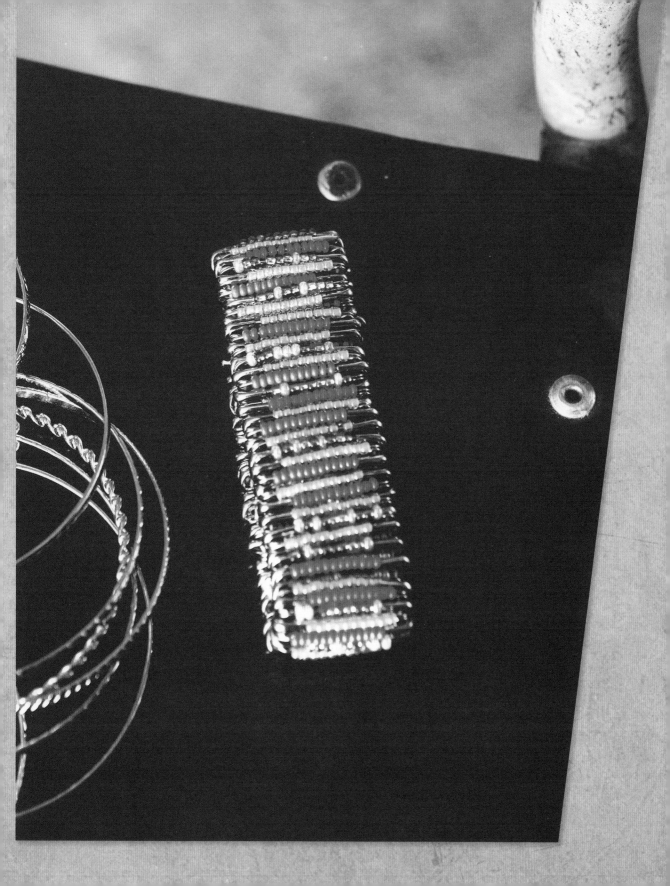

SAILOR KNOT BRACELET

The chunky sailor knot looks much more complex to make than it is, and will create a stunning statement bracelet that you can wear with pride. For an even more bold, dramatic look try working with two colors.

YOU WILL NEED

> THICK CORD, IN TWO COLORS, 45 CM OF EACH

> SCISSORS

> SUPERGLUE

> WIDE RIBBON-END CLASPS, SET OF 2

> FLAT-NOSE JEWELRY PLIERS

> SLIM FLAT-NOSE JEWELRY PLIERS X 2

> JUMP RINGS X 2

> LOBSTER CLASP

CUSTOMIZATION TIP

Use the cord handles from fancy carrier bags for an eco-friendly bargain bracelet. Either mix cords from two bags or use both handles from one bag to make a chic single-color version.

TIE A STRIKING SAILOR KNOT TO MAKE A BRACELET THAT WILL REALLY WOW!

1 Cut the cord to two pieces of the required length. Fold one of the pieces of cord in half and position into a loop with the folded end lying over the tails.

2 Fold the second piece of cord in half and position under the loop of the first cord, with the folded end positioned toward the fold of the first piece of cord.

3 Pass the folded end of the second cord over the folded end of the first piece of cord and then pass it under the tails of the first cord on the left-hand side.

4 Bring the folded ends of the second cord back to the right-hand side, passing it over the first part of the loop of the first cord, under the tails of the second cord, and then back over the second part of the loop of the first cord. Holding the folded ends and tails of cord on either side, carefully draw up to tighten the knot.

5 Trim the ends of the cord to the desired length for your wrist. Apply a small dab of glue to the ends and insert into the wide ribbon-end clasps. Use the flat-nose jewelry pliers to press the clasps closed.

6 Use the two pairs of slim flat-nose pliers to twist open the jump rings. Using the rings, secure the two parts of the lobster clasp into position on the ribbon-end clasps on either side of the bracelet to finish.

QUICK TIP

When opening jump rings to secure the clasp, work carefully. Twist the two sections apart by holding the ends of each section with a set of pliers in each hand and rotate the pliers away from each other. By twisting the rings apart, rather than pulling them open, you will be able to close them back neatly by reversing the process to restore the original perfect circle shape.

QUICK TIP

Use superglue with care to avoid contact with your fingers and clothing. Work in small dabs at a time so that this is not visible on the finished piece.

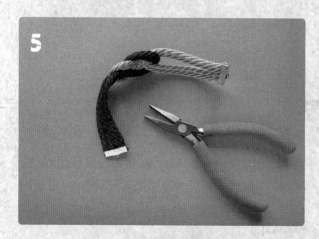

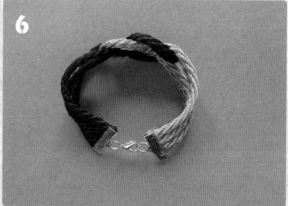

MULTI-STRAND BRAID BRACELET

A simple braid design is enhanced by a combination of shell beads in rich colors and glossy, clear glass beads, creating a dramatic designer-style accessory.

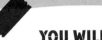

YOU WILL NEED

- TIGER TAIL WIRE, 1.5 M
- JEWELRY WIRE CUTTERS
- SIX-STRAND SLIDE CLASP
- CRIMP BEADS X 18
- FLAT-NOSE JEWELRY PLIERS
- TURQUOISE BEAD CHIPS X 40.6 CM STRAND (APPROX 100 BEADS)
- CORAL BEADS, 4 MM, X APPROX 70
- CLEAR GLASS BEADS, 4 MM, X APPROX 70
- NATURAL COLOR SHELL BEADS X 40.6 CM STRAND (APPROX 90 BEADS)

CUSTOMIZATION TIP

Replace the central two strands of beads with velvet or suede ribbon secured in crimp beads and mix with beads from your stash that harmonize to create your own stylish braided bracelet design. Why not try black velvet ribbon with round pearl and faceted jet beads, or light brown suede ribbon with natural shell and conker brown wood beads?

TEAM SHELL AND GLASS BEADS FOR A STYLISH BRACELET THAT WILL REALLY TURN HEADS!

1 Trim the tiger tail wire into six equal lengths, each measuring 5 cm longer than the desired length for your wrist measurement. Feed through the strand loops on one half of the clasp, slide a crimp bead onto the tiger tail wire, and feed the short end of the tiger tail wire back through the crimp bead to create a loop. Use the flat-nose pliers to press the crimp bead closed to secure the wires in place. Continue to secure all six strands of tiger tail wire into the one half of the clasp with crimp beads. Use the wire cutters to neatly trim away the short excess ends of wire.

2 Working on each strand in turn, thread the selection of beads onto the tiger tail wire. Use the turquoise beads for the first two strands, the coral and the glass beads for the next two strands, and the shell beads on the final two strands.

3 Make sure that all the beaded sections are the same length, then slide a crimp bead onto each length of wire and press closed with the flat-nose pliers to hold the beads neatly in place.

4 Take the outer two strands in toward the center in turn to create a braid. Continue to loosely braid the bracelet for the entire length of the beads.

QUICK TIP

Be careful when using wire cutters: protect your eyes with safety goggles (swimming goggles work well, too) and wear leather gloves, as small sections of wire can be very sharp and may cause injury.

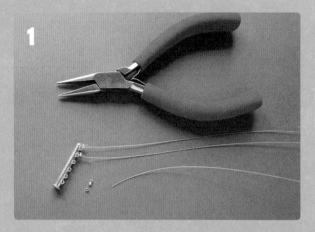

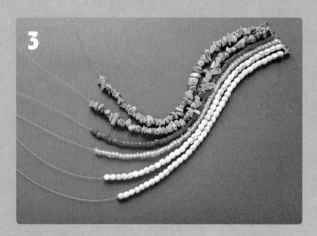

5 Slide a crimp bead onto each of the tiger tail wires before passing through the corresponding strand loops on the second half of the clasp.

6 Drawing the clasp up to the end of the braided section, feed the wire through the corresponding crimp beads in turn and press closed with the flat-nose pliers to secure. Use the wire cutters to neatly cut away the excess wire.

5

6

WIRE WORD BRACELET

Bending and manipulating jewelry wire into a message or the letters of your name is a fun way to create a personalized accessory. Why not make some for your friends, too?

YOU WILL NEED

> MEDIUM-GAUGE JEWELRY WIRE

> JEWELRY WIRE CUTTERS

> ROUND-NOSE JEWELRY PLIERS

> THREE STRANDS OF COLORED CORD AND SUEDE, 10 CM EACH

> SCISSORS

> RIBBON ENDS X 2

> FLAT-NOSE JEWELRY PLIERS

> SLIM FLAT-NOSE JEWELRY PLIERS X 2

> LARGE JUMP RINGS X 3

> LOBSTER CLASP

CUSTOMIZATION TIP

Create your own design using the wire to form your name, a fun word, or a striking motif!

PERSONALIZE YOUR LOOK WITH A WIRE WORD BRACELET!

1 Cut a length of medium-gauge jewelry wire using the jewelry wire cutters. Using the round-nose pliers, create a small coil in the end of the wire. Bend and fold the wire to create your name, word, or motif. Add a second small coil of wire to the other end of the wire and trim away the excess.

2 Cut the cord and suede to length. Secure the ends of the three cord and suede strands into one of the ribbon ends and use the flat-nose pliers to press closed and secure together.

3 Pass the outer cords in toward the center in turn to create a braid. Braid the lengths together, then secure the ends in place with the second ribbon end using the flat-nose pliers.

4 Using the two pairs of slim round-nose jewelry pliers, twist open a jump ring and feed it through the small coil created at the end of the wire word and then through the ribbon end on the braid to join them together. Twist the jump ring back to close neatly.

QUICK TIP

When opening jump rings to secure the clasp, work carefully. Twist the two sections apart by holding the ends of each section with a set of pliers held in each hand, then rotate the pliers away from each other. By twisting the rings apart, rather than pulling them open, you will be able to close them back neatly—just reverse the twist process to restore the original perfect circle shape.

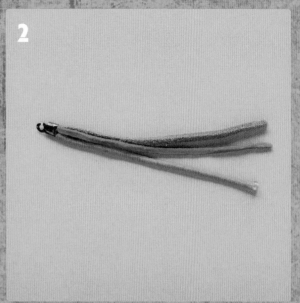

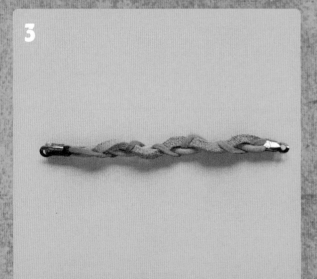

5 Repeat step 4 to add a jump ring to the other coil on the opposite side of the wire word (the beginning of the word).

6 In the same manner, twist open the final jump ring and use it to secure the lobster clasp to the remaining ribbon end on the braided cord.

QUICK TIP

Be careful when using wire cutters: protect your eyes with safety goggles (swimming goggles work well, too) and wear leather gloves, as small sections of wire can be very sharp and may cause injury.

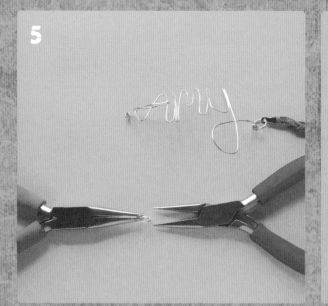

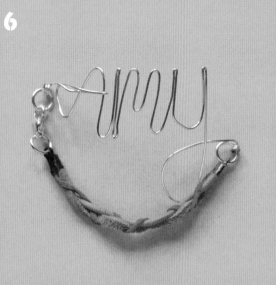

QUICK TIP

Create a guide for bending the wire into a word. Write out your word on paper so that you are happy with how it looks, then use this as a template while bending the wire.

MULTI-STRAND BEADED BRACELET

Memory wire retains its shape, making it a fantastic choice for creating this stacked strand-effect beaded bracelet. Select your favorite color combinations for real stand-out style.

YOU WILL NEED

> JEWELRY WIRE CUTTERS

> MEMORY WIRE

> ROUND-NOSE JEWELRY PLIERS

> SELECTION OF BEADS (AMOUNTS ALL APPROX): GREEN SEED X 250; BLUE GLASS, 4 MM, X 110; CLEAR GLASS, 4 MM, X 60; RED GLASS, 4 MM, X 50; GOLD CUBE, 4 MM, X 7; WHITE CUBE, 4 MM, X 10; LIGHT BLUE GLASS, 4 MM, X 7; OPAQUE BLUE GLASS, 4 MM, X 7; SMALL SILVER, 3 MM, X 7

> JUMP RINGS X 2

> BRACELET TOGGLE CLASP

CUSTOMIZATION TIP

Work with two contrasting colors and create a stacked stripe that runs through the individual strands.

STAND OUT FROM THE CROWD

WITH SPARKLING BEADS!

QUICK TIP

Be careful when using wire cutters and working with memory wire. Protect your eyes with safety goggles (swimming goggles work well, too) and wear leather gloves, as small sections of memory wire can be very sharp and can cause injury.

1 Use the wire cutters to carefully trim the memory wire into 6 lengths that are each 6 cm longer than your desired finished measurement around your wrist.

2 Use the round-nose jewelry pliers to create a small loop in one end of each length of memory wire.

3 Begin feeding the beads onto the lengths of memory wire. The neat end loops will prevent the beads from sliding off.

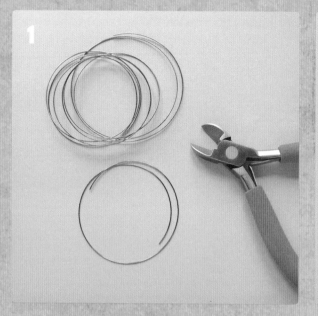

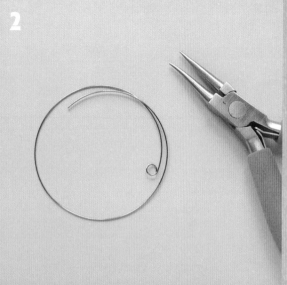

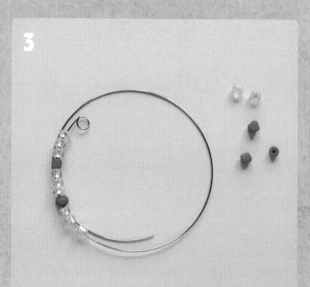

QUICK TIP

When making a wire loop, hold the wire ends level in the pliers, being careful that the ends don't extend above the pliers. Press your thumb on the end of the wire that lies on the pliers and begin rolling the pliers around to make the neat loop. Don't try to do this in one action, or your wrist will end up aching. Simply reposition the pliers and begin rolling again until the loop is finished.

4 Create a different design with the beads on each of the six lengths of memory wire. Work with different colors and shapes of beads to make each length unique.

5 Once you have finished threading beads onto each length, use the round-nose jewelry pliers to create a second small loop in the other end of the lengths of memory wire. This second loop will hold the beads securely in place on the length of wire.

6 Twist open a jump ring (see tip) and feed the loops onto the ends of the memory wires into the ring. Add one half of the bracelet toggle clasp and twist closed (see tip).

7 Repeat with the second jump ring on the other side of the bracelet to join the ends of the strands together and then secure the second half of the bracelet toggle clasp.

QUICK TIP

When opening jump rings to secure the clasp, work carefully. Twist the two sections apart by holding the ends of each section with a set of pliers held in each hand, then rotate the pliers away from each other. By twisting the rings apart, rather than pulling them open, you will be able to close them back neatly—just reverse the twist process to restore the original perfect circle shape.

ZIPPER BRACELET

This simple strip bracelet is created from a standard jeans zipper. The metallic teeth create a dramatic finish to this easy-to-make bracelet, and the slider tab is used to hang a bead dangle.

YOU WILL NEED

- ❭ ZIPPER WITH METAL TEETH, 18 CM
- ❭ SUPERGLUE
- ❭ STATEMENT BEAD
- ❭ GLASS BEADS, 4 MM, IN TWO COLORS, X 6
- ❭ SILVER HEAD PIN
- ❭ ROUND-NOSE JEWELRY PLIERS
- ❭ JEWELRY WIRE CUTTERS
- ❭ SLIM FLAT-NOSE JEWELRY PLIERS X 2
- ❭ JUMP RING X 1
- ❭ LOBSTER CLASP

CUSTOMIZATION TIP

Zipper tapes come in a range of colors and finishes, including a luxurious satin tape. Create a selection of bracelets using different zippers and hanging charms and wear them together for maximum impact.

MAKE AN IMPACT WITH A ZIPPY FASHION BRACELET!

1 With the zipper fastened and teeth placed downward, add a line of superglue to the length of the webbing on one side of the teeth. Fold the webbing over the glue and press in place to create a thin strip. Set aside to allow the glue to dry.

2 Repeat to add a line of superglue along the webbing on the second side of the zipper and fold in to create a thin strip. Set aside to allow the glue to dry.

3 Slide three small beads, the statement bead, and three more glass beads onto the head pin. Use the round-nose pliers to make a neat loop at the end of the head pin and use the wire cutters to trim away the excess wire (see Quick Tip on page 66 for safety advice when working with wire cutters).

4 Use two pairs of the slim flat-nose pliers to twist open the jump ring. Push the ends of the open ring up through either side of the webbing below the closed end of the zipper. Feed on the bead charm and the lobster clasp, then twist closed neatly. Trim away the excess webbing at the zipper tab end and secure the lobster clasp to the slider tab to create the bracelet.

QUICK TIP

When opening jump rings, work carefully. Twist the two sections apart by holding the ends of each section with a set of pliers held in each hand, then rotate the pliers away from each other. By twisting the rings apart, rather than pulling them open, you will be able to close them back neatly— just reverse the twist process to restore the original perfect circle shape.

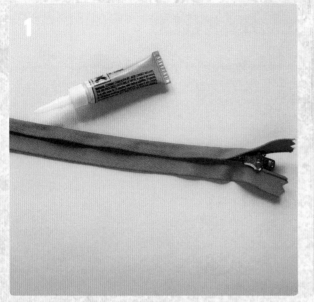

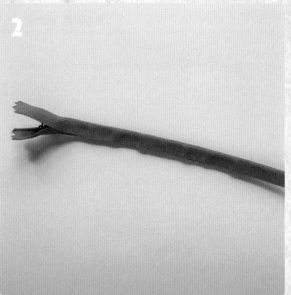

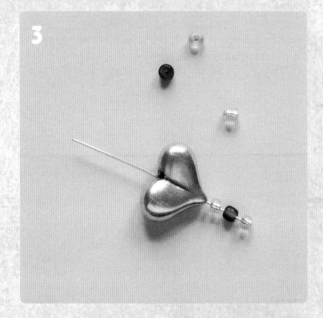

SPRAY PAINT BANGLE

Update your look in an instant with this speedy bracelet makeover. Take an old bangle, team bright acrylic-based spray paints with shining metallic markers, then unleash your creativity!

YOU WILL NEED

> OLD PLASTIC OR WOOD SMOOTH-SURFACED BANGLE

> PAPER TO COVER WORK SURFACE

> ACRYLIC SPRAY PAINT

> METALLIC MARKER

> PENCIL (OPTIONAL)

CUSTOMIZATION TIP

Why not use the metallic markers to add your name (or your friend's name if you are making the bangle as a gift), or a favorite word or a meaningful slogan for a truly personal bracelet!

UPCYCLE OLD BANGLES WITH COLORFUL PAINTS AND MARKERS

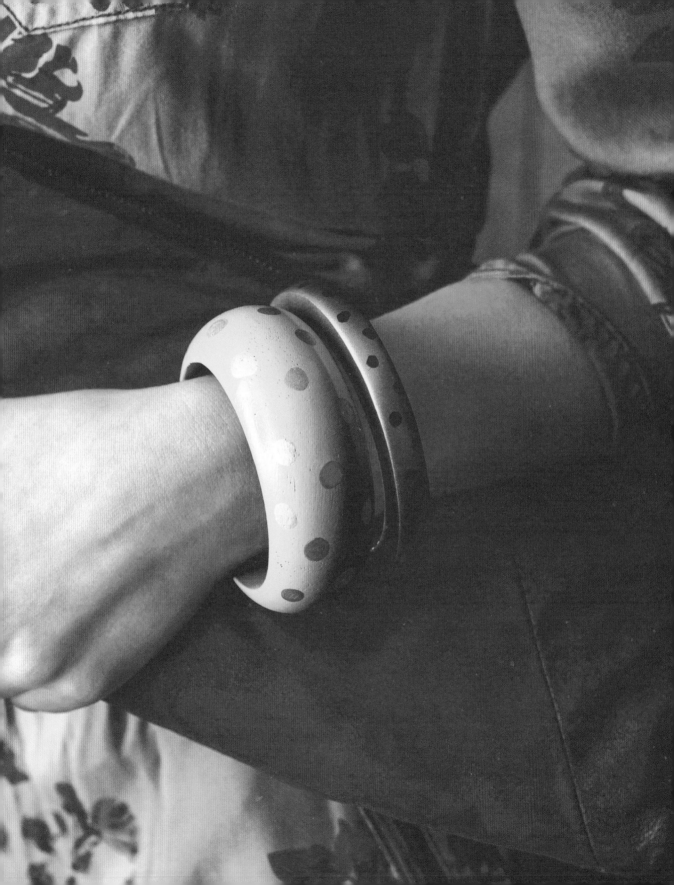

1 Clean the surface of the bangle in soapy water to remove any dust or dirt. Rinse and dry.

2 In a well-ventilated area, cover your work surface with paper to protect it from stray paint. Using an acrylic-based paint, work in small bursts of spray and repeated arching motions to cover the bangle in paint. Allow up to 60 minutes for the paint to become touch dry before painting any remaining sections.

3 Once the paint is fully dry, begin to draw your design using the marker. You may want to sketch the design out in pencil lightly first to give yourself guide lines.

4 Complete the design, working carefully to make sure that you don't touch any of the marker elements until they are fully dry (about 20 minutes), or they may smudge.

QUICK TIP

Only use spray paints in well-ventilated areas, and make sure that all surfaces are covered with protective paper. Wear old clothing so that it doesn't matter if some spray accidentally lands on your jeans instead of the bangle. You could also wear a decorator's protective mask if you are worried about breathing in paint fumes.

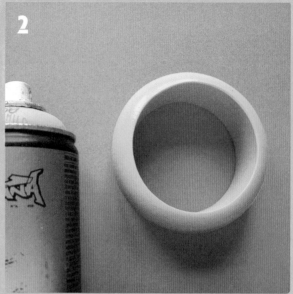

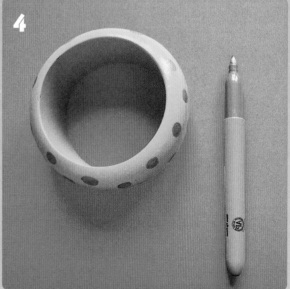

BEADED BRAID BRACELET

A handful of little golden beads and a single statement bead in a pop of contrast color will transform a casual braided cord bracelet design into a stylish party accessory.

YOU WILL NEED

> THIN COTTON CORD, 2 M

> SCISSORS

> SMALL GOLD BEADS, 4 MM, X 42

> LARGE STATEMENT BEAD

CUSTOMIZATION TIP

Mix and match cord and bead colors to create signature style bracelets for every occasion. Why not try black thread, silver beads, and a silver charm instead of a statement bead for a party combination that will go with your little black dress?

METALLIC BEADS ADD A CHIC TOUCH TO A CLASSIC CORD BRACELET

1 Cut the cord to 2 lengths of 1 m each and, holding them together, fold both lengths in half. Tie a knot at the top of the fold to create a small loop through which the statement bead can pass (this will form the fastening for the bracelet).

2 Trim away one of the lengths of cord at the base of the knot and braid the remaining three lengths together for 2 cm. To create a braid, take the outer two strands in toward the center in turn. Tie a knot to secure.

3 Thread a selection of gold beads onto each of the three strands of cord, sliding away from the cut end to prevent them from sliding off.

4 Slide the first bead up the outermost strand of cord on the left-hand side and then bring the cord to the center. Next, slide the first bead of the outermost strand of the cord on the right-hand side and then bring the cord to the center. The beads will be secured at each side of the braid.

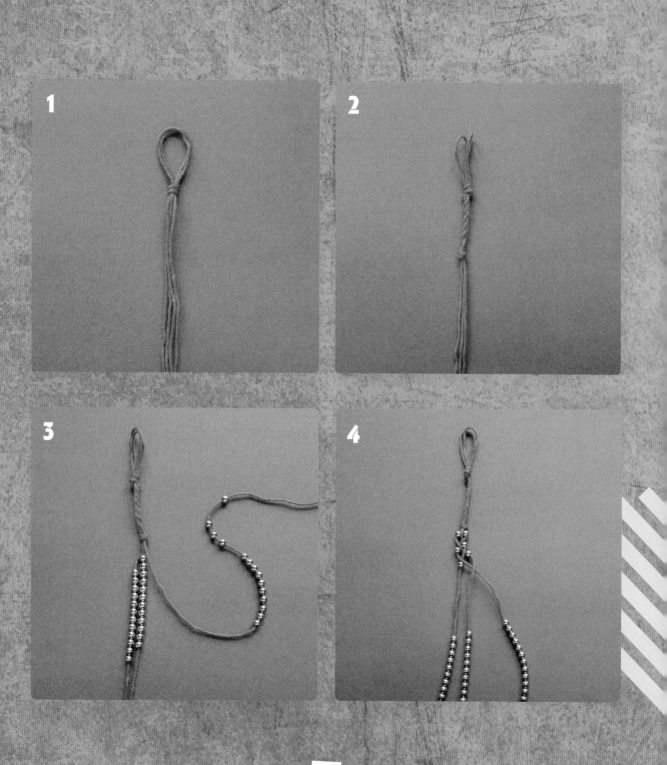

5 Continue braiding the cord, securing a bead at each side with each motion, until the beaded section of the braid is the required length for your wrist, reserving one gold bead to pair with the statement bead.

6 Add a knot to the base of the braid to secure the cord and beads neatly into place.

7 Without adding more beads, braid the remaining free cord for 2 cm, then knot again. Thread the three strands of cord through the statement bead.

8 Add a single bead to the three strands of cord, then knot them together securely to complete the second bracelet tie. Trim the cord below the knot to finish. To wear, wrap around your wrist and pass the statement bead through the loop to secure.

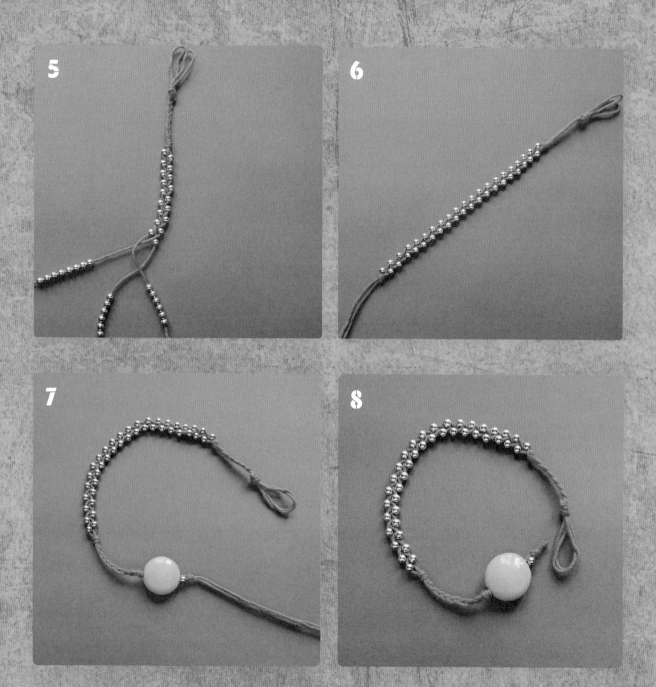

LOOM-BAND BRACELET

Fashionable loom bands are a great way to weave a bright, fun bracelet. This wide bracelet with its striking chevron design gives you plenty of space to use a rainbow of colors.

YOU WILL NEED

› LOOM BANDS IN A RANGE OF COLORS X 6 PACKS

› LOOM-BAND LOOM, LONG

› LOOM-BAND HOOK

› LOOM-BAND FASTENING CLIP

CUSTOMIZATION TIP

Try making a bracelet with even more colors to create a full rainbow, or just stick to two of your favorite shades for a dramatic striped finish.

WHY NOT WEAVE A RAINBOW COLLECTION OF LOOM-BAND BRACELETS?

1 Arrange a selection of loom bands into sets of your chosen colors. Lay them out in the order of your chosen design. This makes constructing the bracelet quick and easy. Positioning the loom-band loom with the indents in the pins facing away from you, begin to place the bands in pairs in strips up the length of the loom. Work upward in three strips, alternating the colors of the bands to create the stripes on the finished bracelet.

2 Turn the loom-band loom around so that the indents in the pins are facing toward you, and begin positioning the center bands. Work across the three strips of positioned loom bands to create small triangles across the loom.

3 Twist a single loom band (black here) into a figure-eight, and position it onto the lowest center pin of the loom. This will become the closure for the bracelet.

4 Starting from the lowest band and working upward, insert the loom-band hook into the indent in the pin behind the central triangle band, and pick up and lift the bands and pass them onto the pin above them.

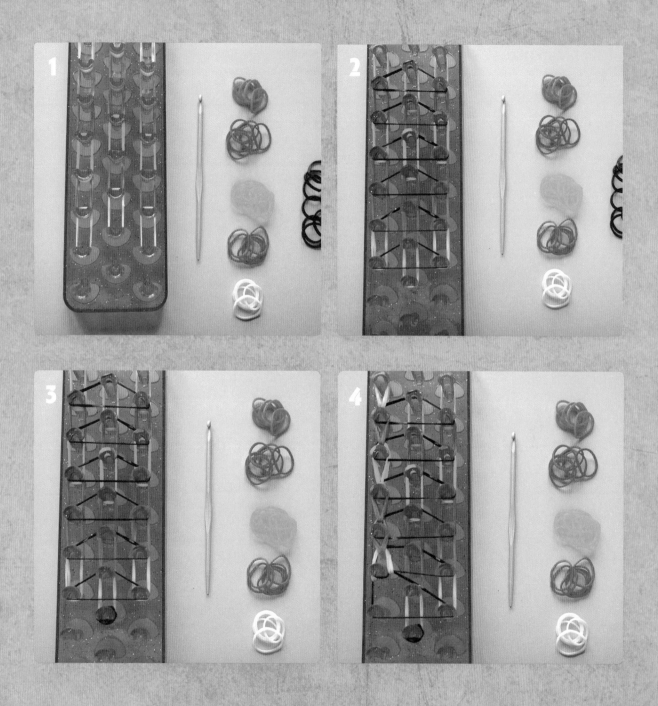

5 Repeat the process to pass the loom bands onto the pin above on the next two rows of bands.

6 Draw the outer two sections of the lowest center triangle loom band into the center, twisting them before placing them onto the center pin on the loom-band loom. This twist will become the second part of the closure for the bracelet.

7 Insert the loom-band fastening into the twisted loom band to secure the fastening. Starting at the secured fastening, carefully begin to lift the bands free from the loom-band loom. Your bracelet is now ready to wear!

8 Secure the second half of the loom-band fastening clips into the small looped loom band on the other side to create the bracelet.

QUICK TIP

The loom-band loom stretches the bands to around double their length while you are creating the design, so you need to make sure that the stripes of bands on the loom are long enough to go around your wrist when you take them off the loom. The stretched length on the loom will need to be double your wrist measurement plus 5 cm for fit.

MATERIALS

All the projects list the materials you need to make them. Some additional advice is provided here.

EMBROIDERY THREAD
Each strand of embroidery floss is usually made up of six fine strands of mercerized cotton, giving the thread a soft, silky feel. You use all the fine strands together as one thread for your bracelet. There are more than 500 color choices on the market, so you'll be able to match your Chevron Friendship Band (see page 8) to any outfit.

CORD
You can find cord in a range of fibers, including nylon, cotton, leather, and faux suede, and in a range of thicknesses. A fine cotton cord is used for the Beaded Braid design (see page 78), fine waxed cotton cord for the Charm Motif Bracelet (see page 14), thicker cord for the Sailor Knot project (see page 48), and chunky paracord for the Urban Knot Bracelet (see page 30). You should always choose the same weight of cord, but you can vary the fiber and color to customize the design.

JEWELRY FINDINGS
Fixtures such as clasps, ribbon ends, and crimp beads are known as jewelry findings. These specialist fittings are available in silver- and gold-tone metal, and also in enameled metal in a range of colors. You can also buy sterling silver findings for a special project.

SEED BEADS
Also known as rocailles, these tiny glass beads resemble little seeds, hence the name. Japanese or Czech in origin, they are available in a huge range of colors. Japanese beads have a larger hole and are more regular in shape, but are also more costly.

WIRE
Steel memory wire is used for the Multi-strand Beaded Bracelet (see page 64) as it holds its curved shape easily. Sold in coils, it is often plated to give a silver, gold, or antique brass effect. This wire is very hard, so you will need to use wire cutters designed for cutting memory wire. Jewelry wire is softer and easy to bend, so it is ideal for the Wire Word Bracelet (see page 58). It's usually made from silver-plated copper, though enameled versions are also available in a range of colors (use nylon-jawed pliers with these so you don't mark the wire as you bend it).

JEWELRY PLIERS
You will need both flat-nose and round-nose types for the projects in this book. Round-nose pliers have jaws that taper to a point and are ideal for making loops. Position

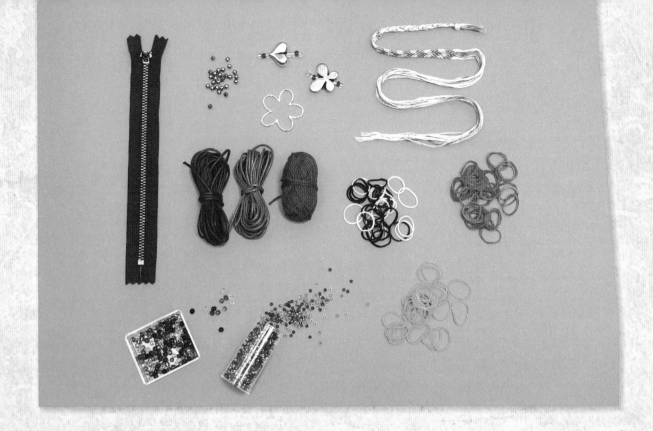

your wire near the handle for a large loop and near the tip of the jaws for a small loop. Flat-nose types have jaws that don't taper, and are used for opening and closing jump rings and gripping wire.

LOOM BANDS
The bands are generally made of silicone rather than rubber, which is good news for those allergic to latex. There's a huge range of colors and special finishes, such as pearlized or metallic hues, available.

ACRYLIC SPRAY PAINT
Always use decorative spray paints in a well-ventilated area and cover surfaces in the immediate area. You may want to wear old clothes and disposable gloves, too. Hold the can around 25 cm away from the bangle and move it back and forth in an even manner. Paint will be touch dry in around an hour (though fast-dry types will be touch dry in 10 minutes) and fully dry the next day. You can find a range of colors, including metallic effects.

WASHI TAPE
This sticky tape, as used in the Washi Tape Bangle (see page 26), is essentially a decorative masking tape that originated in Japan and has become a very popular material for a number of crafts, including card making, scrapbooking, gift wrapping, and jewelry making—to name just a few!

CHARMS
The addition of charms is a quick and easy way to customize a project, such as the Zipper Bracelet (see page 70), or can be used as a focal point, such as the Charm Motif Bracelet (see page 14). These motifs in all shapes and sizes are usually found in the jewelry section of craft stores—or you can make your own accents with selections of beads and jewelry wire.

RESOURCES

If you are a keen crafter, you will probably have some of the tools and materials for the projects in this book already—and a few of the projects, like the T-shirt Yarn Bracelet (see page 20), simply upcycle things you will have around the home. If you need to buy more specialist items, such as the jewelry pliers or memory wire, you'll find pretty much everything you need at large craft stores. If you can't find anything at your local store, there's a huge range of online suppliers with an amazing choice of beads and other bits and bobs. There are lots of wonderful online specialist sources for jewelry supplies, though you might like to browse for beads at a brick and mortar store if you get the chance, as the experience of choosing from a treasure chest of styles you can touch and feel will inspire you.

AC Moore

www.acmoore.com
While they don't sell products online (only in-store), AC Moore's website offers a plethora of project ideas and inspiration.

Ben Franklin Crafts

www.benfranklinartsandcrafts.com
This chain of independently owned stores offers a wide breadth of products for you to peruse. While you can't purchase online, their website contains craft videos for inspiration.

CreateForLess

www.createforless.com
An online-only shop, CreateForLess.com offers great prices on a range of crafting supplies.

Fire Mountain Gems and Beads

www.firemountaingems.com
This online retailer offers wholesale prices on "billions" of beads and other jewelry-making supplies.

Hobby Lobby

www.shop.hobbylobby.com
With over 60,000 products, Hobby Lobby is sure to have just what you need for your jewelry-making endeavors.

Joann Fabrics

www.joann.com
Known primarily for its fabric supplies, Joann Fabrics will also amaze you with their selection of jewelry-making products.

Michaels

www.michaels.com
This North American craft store chain has thousands of products ranging from jewelry-making supplies to art essentials.

M&J Trimmings

www.mjtrim.com
This New York–based store offers a wide selection online and ships internationally. Their inventory includes Swarovski crystals and beautiful pendants.

INDEX

ABOUT THE AUTHOR

Laura Strutt is a craft designer and maker living in Colchester, UK, with her husband as well as her little dog, Waffle. She is the author of a number of crafting books, including some on sewing, wedding, and yarn crafts. Laura regularly teaches at workshops around the UK and shares lots of creative projects, how-to guides, recipes, and crafty inspiration on her website *www.madepeachy.com.*

ACKNOWLEDGMENTS

Creating these arm candy designs for this book has been a lot of fun—there is nothing more inspiring than being surrounded by lots of brightly colored beads, trinkets, charms, and findings! There have been a number of people who have contributed to the creation of this book, and thanks goes out to them all. In particular, Amy Christian at Pavilion Books for commissioning such a fantastic and fun book, and Judith More for her fabulous attention to detail. Finally, special thanks to my husband, John Strutt, for his endless support, creative input, and tolerance to being surrounded by crafty supplies 24/7!

Step-by-step photography by Laura Strutt
Main project photography by Christina Wilson